THE USBORNE EASTER STORY

Retold by Heather Amery

Designed and illustrated by Norman Young

Language consultant: Betty Root
Series editor: Jenny Tyler

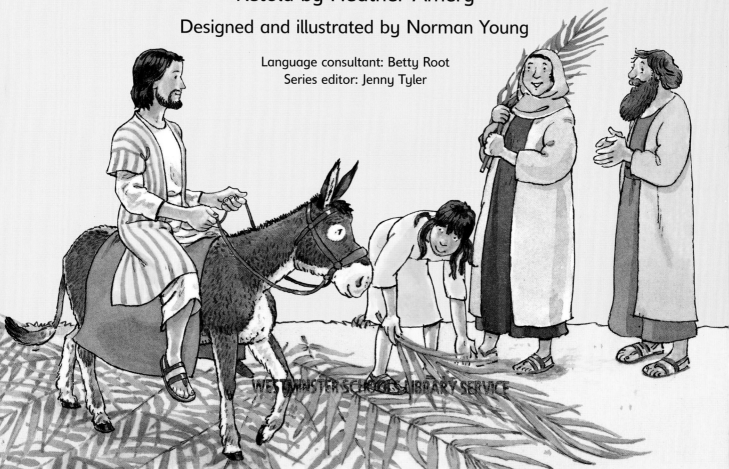

Jesus went to Jerusalem.

He rode into the great city of Jerusalem on a donkey. His twelve disciples walked along with him.

The people cheered Jesus.

They cut down palms and laid them on the road.
They had heard he was their new leader.

That night Jesus had a special supper.

Jesus told his twelve disciples that he would die soon. Judas, one of the disciples, left the room.

Jesus broke up some bread.

He gave a piece to each disciple. "This is my body which I give for you," he said.

Jesus picked up a cup of wine.

"This is my blood. I give it for you and all people," he said. Each disciple drank wine from the cup.

Then Jesus went to a garden to pray.

Eleven disciples went with him. Judas had gone to tell the enemies of Jesus where to find him.

Soldiers came to arrest Jesus.

The Temple priests accused Jesus of saying he was a king. They said he had broken the laws of God.

They were afraid of Jesus.

They thought Jesus wanted all the people to fight
against them and their Roman rulers.

9

They took Jesus to the Roman Governor.

The priests told him lies about Jesus. The Governor didn't want Jesus to be killed but he agreed.

The soldiers beat Jesus.

Then they made him carry a heavy cross up a hill.
He was very tired and often fell down.

They nailed Jesus to a cross.

They put it up with two other crosses. Jesus's mother and his friends were there.

Jesus died at midday on Friday.

That evening, a friend called Joseph took Jesus away. He put him in a tomb on a hill.

Mary, a friend of Jesus's, went to the tomb.

It was early on Sunday morning. Mary looked in the tomb. It was empty. Jesus was gone.

Mary spoke to a man.

"Where have you taken Jesus?" she said. "Mary,"
said the man. Mary saw he was Jesus.

"Jesus is alive."

Mary ran to tell his friends. They were very happy. They often saw Jesus before he went to Heaven.

This edition first published in 2005 by Usborne Publishing Ltd, 83-85 Saffron Hill, London EC1N 8RT, England. www.usborne.com
Copyright © 2005, 2004, 1999, 1998, 1997 Usborne Publishing Ltd. The name Usborne and the devices ♀ ⊕ are Trade Marks
of Usborne Publishing Ltd. All rights reserved. No part of this publication may be reproduced, stored in a retrieval system, or transmitted
in any form or by any means, electronic, mechanical, photocopying, recording or otherwise, without the prior permission of the publisher. UE
First published in America 2005. Printed in China.